Mental Minutiae

George K. Karos II

ISBN: 978-81-8253-878-8

First Edition: 2022
Rs. 200/-

Cyberwit.net
HIG 45 Kaushambi Kunj, Kalindipuram
Allahabad - 211011 (U.P.) India
http://www.cyberwit.net
Tel: +(91) 9415091004
E-mail: info@cyberwit.net

Printed at Thomson Press India Limited.

Contents

*

Will you understand these statements?
The pleas from which they're intended.

Belligerent acts of aggression
carried out through uncertain terror.

Pathetic portrayals of brutality
tolerated for the dominance of others.

We of human fleeting flesh,
imperfect juncture and selection?

Protests around the world,
an ongoing sequence of events.

With and without regions
of unchartered interplanetary formulation.

With and without solemn recollections
of unfulfilled visions.

A unison of condemnations
constantly originating in foreign homelands.

Skirmishes instigated by the threat
of unfamiliar persons.

I chose the hopeful pathway
of every waking moment.

I channel ancestral neglects
to restore humanity's merciful purpose.

*

We endured an enforced pause
in response to a worldwide pandemic.

Inspired by dread, we questioned
our motivations of much we had previously pursued.

That of egocentric self-regard
and covetous extravagances.

That of perceived petty phantoms
digitized through mass media.

That of visual packages of propagandas
reinforcing disgusting habits obliging self-absorptions.

Devious manipulations overcome by the compulsions
to exploit those we branded neighbors, friends, and family.

*

We are all part of designated tourism industries.

Baring longstanding guilt
from never exploring
new directions in travel.

Slouching, repeating, devising strategies
seeking someone, or anything to agree with.

Embracing divergences
overlooked on a regular basis.

Hyperbole yielding
to positive existences
never noticed entirely.

We are all part of designated tourism industries.

Chartered trips voyaged
through outliers of realities.

Rejoicing in the grace of targeted joys
or the most incredible of devastations.

Gathering nearby infinite seashores
trailing the sorted sounds of animal echoes.

Visitors vying together
with an unsheltered natural world
neither anyone's nor anything's.

*

Our collective fates
depend upon
never trivializing
decency embraced
versus decency appreciated.

Our addiction to contempt
has emptied our better minds
and derailed our critical thinking
causing us to be slaves to binary choices:

Black: white
Left; right

acquainting us with the dated notion
that our lives are far more complicated
than two-fold options of limited engagement
designed to influence our fantastic freedoms:

modulating; space
allowing; forward motion.

*

Tenderness validates my intuitive responses to delight.

*In either the fusion of kindheartedness
or heart wrenching of gloom.*

Tenderness validates my intuitive responses to delight.

*By either establishing a brutal indulgence,
or constructing an empathy of truth.*

Tenderness validates my intuitive responses to delight.

*Acknowledging harmony, or peace
amid existence's impermanence.*

*

Unnamable and able mystery,
I call upon you to manifest
your forbearing self to me.

Within the boundaries
of your dignified grace
I have remained ungrateful.
Cleanse the woes of my mind
through your lenient blessings.

Superabundant companion of life and death,
through your unceasing brilliance
please receive my humble prayers
seeking the bravery to humbly emulate
your immense compassion throughout all my life.

*

*Seeking to participate in suppressive relationships,
my contradictions are too bountiful to mention.*

*I recognize entirety, continually fading,
has also dawned before.*

*

To live both asleep and woken
I fail by my own standards.

Thoughtlessly, I have allowed my essence
to be guided by avidity.

But through you, most merciful divine,
I continue to seek your blessing.

Ripened by the forbearing radiance
befalling ages before me.

Awarding me apt fruits
of wholehearted benevolence.

Me, a loathsome and frivolous being of persona,
Me, seeking supervision from the source of all substance.

Through you, the most generous potential of hopefulness.
In you, lies all the love and lenience I could ever endeavor
to obtain.

*

Inhabiting immeasurable darkness
ill-disposed and unearthing
an incandescence at the core
of wherever warmness
becomes hotness
eventually.

Established separately
measured urgently
by accelerated realms
of oblivious uncertainty
sharing each other's
stratosphere.

*

Can anyone be helped
as much as they need
in any given scenario
where ego-driven actors
force ill-willed confrontations?

May we allow assistance
in aliquant proportionality
to be more supportive in time
then when evaluated in hindsight.

*

Is every item you bear
an object or story starter?

In any given situation
you have everything you need
to consider success or failure.

We are all merely parents
to the entire universe
around our countless bodies.

*

Mental minutia multiplies
as an enormous expanse
of subjective perspective
emerging within me.

I've tried to consider
the modulations
of short-term notions
once roaming this sphere.

Meeting their schedules
and paying costly debts
before relinquishing their bouts
while still continuously caring.

As Jesus did,
laughing at Judas,
hanging on wooden cross
ridiculed and suffering.

*

Nothing worth bothering anyone about.

*Decades of alienation
from most all of humanity.*

*Over fifty years in prolonged predicaments
demobilized by incarnate love sought
through countless collective relations.*

Nothing worth bothering anyone about.

*Moments engulfed me
as a chronic protagonist.*

*Where I felt unwelcomed
in divinity's awing acts
granting nature's chosen outcome.*

*

Musing, I yield to shallow illusions
of several sensed adversities

sometimes entrusting me
with an astounding and playful poem.

*

Upward and beyond
before and after
every documented century
on the brink of demise.

What can be known of affection
can be perceived as severe
or absurdly restorative
in its tedious mending process.

Generosity between individuals expands
within the most despicable of civilization's creations.

Imperfectly embodying the magnificence
of Divinity's abiding clemency.

*

*Humanity in the world has lessened
as derogatory behaviors have increased
supporting narcissistic lives
catering to either the criminally poor
or ones honorably wealthy.*

*Humanity in the world has lessened
as our desire to belong separate
afterwards, or before, we became
worlds we uniquely loved
or ultimately destroyed.*

*

Starting.
Ending.

Revelations determine perceived advice
on how to advance or terminate flows
leading me, or impeding me,
in any given situation
receiving altogether
what once was secluded
as a momentary pampered union
depending on a condition balanced previously
in any varied progression that familiarizes me.

Starting.
Ending.

*

This is the one true lessen I have learned:
Accept people as they are.

Persons will either find an enthusiasm
to exchange affirmative energies
or disregard your social courtesy.

And be not impolite, my lessen does also conclude.
Except when needing to wane
so never to be thought of once more.

Let us help to make clean
that which is needed cleansed
by aiding behavior of compassionate appeal.

*

Occasionally,
I feel like a traumatized caveman
writing poems about distressing incidents.

An oral infection limited my lyrical output capacities
until healing afterwards, mostly,
when my speech improved steadily
and the words within my worlds
flowed easier and more smoothly.

I'm again humbled to have obtained
vital primeval rejuvenated brainwaves
allowing healthier communication to exist.

Occasionally,
I feel like a traumatized caveman
writing poems about distressing incidents.

*

Let's share
both our hunger and thirst.

Hunger –
the prevailing force that limits ambition.
Thirst –
realizing that seeking supremacy ultimately leads to down-
falls.

Let's share
both our hunger and thirst.

*

Lady Liberty's torch expended

when economic disparity
sprouted without resistance
to F.D.R.'s cozy bonds
with southern governors,
or later when
Reagan's wealth
never trickled down
to reach the domestic shores
of hoodwinked workers
deprived of their labor's pensions.

Lady Liberty's torch expended

When lamenting lives lived
became lost in her lantern's light
shorn over freedom's tense waters
of radicalized people whose flailed flags
of propagandist slogans no longer convey,
"Give us your tired, your poor,
your huddles masses yearning to breathe free."

*

One may search for equity and diversity.
No computer applications can be developed
to create immediate shared experiences.

No law can govern
the prejudiced temperaments
of the many afflicted identities
gaining a healthier perspective
in circumstances experienced subjectively.

Focus one's compassion
across the spheres
of all colors, creeds, and principles?

If so, one may cautiously rejoice
self-aware of the indifferences
between our critical thinking
and mutual multiplicities
void of biased assumptions.

*

Through we, I.
Please, do not interpret my personality as yourself.
I will remind myself to do the same.

Through we, I.
Never try and modify a stranger's politics
of thought or communication.

Through we, I.
Always permit their views to seethe
and reveal reminiscences of times
important enough to remember now.

Through we, I.
Trending towards silence allowing our freedom.
As we all become the darkness of Earth.
Or the bountiful luminous of interstellar space.

*

In disagreement,
become strong and firm
but always polite.

Bare no grudges
but try and remain certain
of your stances.

If respect extended towards differences of opinion
are ignored, willingly, or without unbiased reasons,

then forces that protect conflict
will override all explanations

of why any disparity would ever exist
from ever emerging into slight devastation.

*

Your face resting on my chest
awakens guarded discernments
of threatening abandonments
mutating and variating our mutual desires.

Your exquisite hazel eyes welcome me
to explore better versions of myself
reassessed by subdued self-management
sanctioning our every fond interchange.

*

*A wildly airborne cicada shattered itself
onto the withered forehead of a homeless teenager
tranquilly napping on a shaded Tampa Florida, city side-
walk.*

*Awoken by the insect's destruction upon her face,
as gushing streams of blood bleeding relentlessly
onto her T-shirt's shrill neckline's collar,*

*she wiped her gory brows and drowsy eyelids
groaning slightly, but void of ill-tempered response,
uninterruptedly slouched despondently*

*on her current concrete land-dwelling
knowing this recent bewildering disturbance
would only last for moments.*

*

I have travelled to towns and cities
containing people forgotten and lied to.

Mourning deaths and sufferings
of people they never knew.

And whose meager hardships
selflessly yielded considerations.

More affirmative paths
of permanency.

*

Summer sunset's blue sky's haziness
allows confirmatory rays of confidence

to enter our presence inherently
to help heal our vast debilities

as we breath air carefully
and exhale so conditionally.

*

Question: Who should we vote for?
Answer: An older politician's lies,
or the lies of a newer politician.

Another mass shooting, over 200 this year.
Are we immune to murder?

This time, six people grotesquely mutilated.
How long has this gross conduct been occurring?

As a nation our silence created
sinister community alliances void of caring.

Allowing exploding metal to detonate
on citizens unwell and bloodthirsty indifferent.

Residents seduced by excessive wages
listlessly adapt to monstruous cultural entropies.

Propagandist ideas financed by modes of media insanities
we all seem to cooperatively embrace and champion.

*

Destroyers never defeated.
I adopted friends and family
in lieu of those who were absent.

They were as phantastic
as the ones they replaced.
Persisting in silence I remained.

Destroyers never defeated.
It has been the easiest things
we ever accomplished.

Evading the vindictiveness
perpetrated amongst each other.
Maintaining a disinterest towards each other.

Destroyers never defeated.
The infinite rejection of celestial union seems unreasoned.
Thinking things will somehow work out.

Different generations after novel generations.
Remaining reflective in a state of vanity.
We have all sorrowed while hurting one another.

*

*I've wondered
what a blessing is
in every moment lived.*

*And it is a merciful gift
void of desperation, sadness,
or pompous reluctancy.*

*I've wondered
what a blessing is
in every moment lived,*

*and it is a merciful gift
without anxiety, pressure, or depression
allowing me to remain humble enough to receive.*

*

Take nothing from me
as I offer you favors
of time and company.
Offer nothing to me.
As I receive ruminations
plentiful enough to fit on this page.

Philosophy or religion,
it is our clear choosing to embrace.

Beliefs arguably controlled,
one shorn of punishment,
the other supervised by faith.

Born of mother's suffering
without fathers and whose sons often killed,
or sometimes healed by our combined history's fiction.

Take nothing from me
as I offer you favors
of time and company.
Offer nothing to me.
As I receive ruminations
plentiful enough to fit on this page.

*

Somehow the same moment all these years.

Within worldwide evolutions.
Continuous unvarying intervals.

A worn timepiece turned 360-degree rotations
until it can't be wound any further.

Somehow the same moment all these years.

*

I have grown panic-stricken
about being trivialized
by myself
and others.

I am a failure in my own eyes
but especially in yours
as I perceive
you in me.

I have grown weary of sharing
my insufficient conceptions of love
existing in thoughts, and prayers
as an infallible sense of nothingness
distresses me knowing you
are the only grace I can affirm.

Please never discourage
my humble pursuit
of your perpetual compassion.

*

An honored, now elderly soldier, was once asked:

"Do you like to speak about what you feel?
Or do you prefer to speak about what you think?"

To which she equitably replied,

"I like to speak of both. I feel and think it appears I was denied a family.
By the powers that be. Who thought I'd be better off serving the public?
As no one had ever seen before."

*

It's not very interesting.
It's predictable.
It's eventual.

The ways we avoid the palters
manipulating various truths
in-between relations
that have changed in time.

It's not very interesting.
It's predictable.
It's eventual.

The significant objectifications
that define subsistence and extinction
without living each other's lives
or having shared experiences.

*

Despicable dispositions
in which we often maneuver
dole out slight provisions

for progress to contend
with the deceivers among us
confirming our rare repulsions

with their tireless oppositions
to valuing living's lenience
we all ration unassumingly.

*

*Between every assumption
within perceptions intertwined
rests my wavering attention
devoid of conscience thoughts
or reverie's biased notions
accompanied by realms operating
in contiguous reverberations
emersed in involuntary breaths
drawn in and too soon blown out.*

*

You hide
from me
your need to flee
your sense of community
of where you once were so proud to be
but where now means totally nothing.

*

Pleasant periods overcome me
granted poem after poem
in blank verse
or free verse
to be read
either then
or now.

*

The compulsion to purchase
the items we cherish

initiate mindful dialogues
of supply and demand economically

Diverging merchandises
wholesaled to one

simultaneously augmenting
the value of another.

*

Our minds
are minds
inside other minds
formulating conceptions
from onset until demise
of momentary existences.

Our words
are words
within other words
overly conversed
in solo discussions
with multiple communities.

Our intents
are intents
within recurring intents
modulating sounds and stimuli
readily or unwillingly meant
then, now, or for evermore.

*

*Territorial
telepathies
take hold
of nervous encounters
in between words heard
sometimes questioned
with embarrassing comportment
emitting a madness only grace can console.*

*

Becoming
something
or someone

comprises various times
we've lived and then died
in flesh or trembling moments

that arrived then freely departed
hesitating to respond to stimuli
every hour upon gracious hour.

www.ingramcontent.com/pod-product-compliance
Lightning Source LLC
LaVergne TN
LVHW051455180726
843512LV00001B/35